...ing

Novels for Students, Volume 7

Staff

Series Editor: Deborah A. Stanley.

Contributing Editors: Sara L. Constantakis, Catherine L. Goldstein, Motoko Fujishiro Huthwaite, Arlene M. Johnson, Erin White.

Editorial Technical Specialist: Karen Uchic.

Managing Editor: Joyce Nakamura.

Research: Victoria B. Cariappa, *Research Team Manager*. Andy Malonis, *Research Specialist*. Tamara C. Nott, Tracie A. Richardson, and Cheryl L. Warnock, *Research Associates*. Jeffrey Daniels, *Research Assistant*.

Permissions: Susan M. Trosky, *Permissions Manager*. Maria L. Franklin, *Permissions Specialist*. Sarah Chesney, *Permissions Associate*.

Production: Mary Beth Trimper, *Production Director*. Evi Seoud, *Assistant Production*

Manager. Cindy Range, *Production Assistant*.

Graphic Services: Randy Bassett, *Image Database Supervisor*. Robert Duncan and Michael Logusz, *Imaging Specialists*. Pamela A. Reed, *Photography Coordinator*. Gary Leach, *Macintosh Artist*.

Product Design: Cynthia Baldwin, *Product Design Manager*. Cover Design: Michelle DiMercurio, *Art Director*. Page Design: Pamela A. E. Galbreath, *Senior Art Director*.

of this work have added value to the underlying factual material herein through one or more of the following: unique and original selection, coordination, expression, arrangement, and classification of the information. All rights to this publication will be vigorously defended.

ISBN 0-7876-3826-9
ISSN 1094-3552

Printed in the United States of America.
10 9 8 7 6 5 4 3 2 1

1984

George Orwell

1949

Introduction

Published in 1948 and set thirty-six years in the future, *1984* is George Orwell's dark vision of the future. Written while Orwell was dying and based on the work of the Russian author Yevgeny Zamyatin, it is a chilling depiction of how the power of the state could come to dominate the lives of individuals through cultural conditioning. Perhaps the most powerful science fiction novel of the twentieth century, this apocalyptic satire shows with grim conviction how Winston Smith's individual personality is wiped out and how he is recreated in the Party's image until he does not just obey but even loves Big Brother. Some critics have related Winston Smith's sufferings to those Orwell underwent at preparatory school, experiences he wrote about just before *1984*. Orwell maintained that the book was written with the explicit intention "to alter other people's idea of the kind of society they should strive after."

Author Biography

George Orwell was born Eric Arthur Blair in Bengal, India, in 1903, into a middle-class family. The son of a British civil servant, Orwell was brought to England as a toddler. The boy became aware of class distinctions while attending St. Cyprian's preparatory school in Sussex, where he received a fine education but felt out of place. He was teased and looked down upon because he was not from a wealthy family. This experience made him sensitive to the cruelty of social snobbery.

As a partial-scholarship student whose parents could not afford to pay his entire tuition, Orwell was also regularly reminded of his lowly economic status by school administrators. Conditions improved at Eton, where he studied next, but instead of continuing with university classes, in 1922 he joined the Indian Imperial Police. Stationed in Burma, his class-consciousness intensified as he served as one of the hated policemen enforcing British control of the native population. Sickened by his role as imperialist, he returned to England in 1927 and resigned his position. He planned to become a writer, a profession in which he had not before shown much interest.

In 1928, perhaps to erase guilt from his colonial experiences, he chose to live amongst the poor of London, and later, Paris. In Paris, he published articles in local newspapers, but his fiction was rejected. His own life finally provided the material for his first book, published in 1933. *Down and Out in Paris and London*, which combined fictional narrative based on his time spent in those two cities with social criticism, was his first work published as George Orwell. The pseudonym was used so his parents would not be shocked by the brutal living conditions described in the book. The next year, Orwell published *Burmese Days*, a novel based on his stay in Burma. Subsequent novels contain autobiographical references and served as vehicles for Orwell to explore his growing political convictions.

In 1936, Orwell traveled to Barcelona, Spain, to write about the Spanish Civil War and ended up joining the battle, fighting against Spanish leader Francisco Franco on the side of the Republicans. Wounded, he returned to England. Two nonfiction books, *The Road to Wigan Pier*, a report on deplorable conditions in the mining communities of northern England, and *Homage to Catalonia*, the story of his participation in the Spanish Civil War, allowed Orwell to explicitly defend his political ideas. Dozens of pointed essays also revealed his political viewpoint.

By that time, Orwell clearly saw himself as a political performer whose tool was writing. He wrote in a 1946 essay, "Why I Write," that "every line of serious work that I have written since 1936 has been written, directly or indirectly, *against* totalitarianism and *for* democratic socialism, as I understand it."

Orwell's next book, *Animal Farm*, a fable about the events during and following the Russian Revolution, was well liked by critics and the public. He had had trouble finding a publisher during World War II because the work was a disguised criticism of Russia, England's ally at the time. When it was finally published, just after the war, however, it was a smashing success.

The money Orwell made from *Animal Farm* allowed him, in 1947, to rent a house on Jura, an island off the coast of Scotland, where he began to work on *1984*. His work was interrupted by treatment for tuberculosis, which he had contracted in the 1930s, and upon his release from the hospital in 1948 Orwell returned to Jura to complete the book. Under doctor's orders to work no more than one hour a day, but unable to find a typist to travel to his home, he typed the manuscript himself and collapsed upon completion of the book. For the next two years he was bedridden. Many critics claim that Orwell's failing health may have influenced the tone and outcome of the novel, and Orwell admitted that they were probably right.

Orwell did plan to write other books, according to his friends, and married while in the hospital, but three months later in 1950 he finally died of tuberculosis.

Plot Summary

Part One

In George Orwell's *1984* Winston Smith, a member of the Outer Party from Oceania (a fictional state representing both England and America), lives in all visible ways as a good party member, in complete conformance with the wishes of Big Brother—the leader of the Inner Party (Ingsa). He keeps his loathing for the workings of the Party—for the vile food and drink, the terrible housing, the conversion of children into spies, the orchestrated histrionics of the Two Minutes' Hate—deep inside, hidden, for he knows that such feelings are an offense punishable by death, or worse. But, as the year 1984 begins, he has decided, against his better judgment, to keep a diary in which his true feelings are laid bare. He sits back in an alcove in his dingy apartment, just out of view of the telescreen (two-way television screens that are in all buildings and homes, which broadcast propaganda and transmit back the activities of anyone passing in front of the screen) and writes of his hatred for Big Brother.

Winston works at the Ministry of Truth (Minitrue, in Newspeak), the branch of the government responsible for the production and dissemination of all information. Winston's job is to alter or "rectify" all past news articles which have since been "proven" to be false. Only once has he ever held in his hands absolute proof that the Ministry was lying. It concerned three revolutionaries, Jones, Aaronson, and Rutherford, who were executed for planning a revolt against the state. Winston found evidence that their confessions were falsified and out of fear he destroyed that evidence.

One day during a Two Minutes' Hate session, Winston catches the eye of O'Brien, a member of the Inner Party who seems to carry the same disillusionment about the Party that Winston harbors. Winston realizes that all the stories told by the Party about Emmanuel Goldstein—the head of an underground conspiracy to overthrow the Party —and the traitorous Brotherhood are at least partly true. Perhaps there is another way, and he begins to see hope in the proletariat. They are the 85% of the population of Oceania that exists outside the Party, kept in a perpetual state of slovenly poverty but mostly unregulated, unobserved.

Winston's wanderings among the proles, desperately searching for that little bit of hope, take him one evening to the junk shop where he purchased his diary. The proprietor, Mr. Charrington, Shows him a back room outfitted with a bed, where he and his wife used to live before the Revolution. And there is no telescreen—the proles aren't required to have them.

As he leaves the shop, Winston notices that he is being watched. A dark-haired woman from the fiction department at Minitrue was spying on him.

Fearing the worst, Winston contemplates killing her, but instead he quickly heads home.

Part Two

Winston sees the dark-haired girl at the Ministry of Truth. She stumbles, and as he helps her up, she passes a slip of paper into his hand. Winston reads it in secret and discovers that it is a note saying that she loves him. Lonely and intrigued by her, he manages to eat lunch one day with her. They make plans for another such accidental meeting that evening. In the midst of a crowd, she gives him a complex set of directions to a place where they will meet on Sunday afternoon.

Winston and the girl—Julia—meet in the woods, far out in the country, away from the telescreens. There they are actually able to talk and make love. Julia reveals that she is not what she appears; she despises the Party, but pretends to be a good party member.

The couple meets at irregular intervals, and never in the same place, until Winston suggests the idea of renting Mr. Charrington's room. The two meet, sharing the delicacies that Julia gets on the black market (delicacies like sugar, milk, and real coffee) and relishing their moments of freedom. Their bliss is interrupted only once by the presence of a rat. Julia chases it off and prevents it from coming back.

O'Brien, under the guise of having a copy of the newest Newspeak dictionary, approaches

Winston at the ministry and invites him to his apartment. Winston believes he has a friend and agrees to go with Julia. When Winston and Julia finally do appear, O'Brien assures them that Goldstein and the conspiracy to overthrow the Party do indeed exist, that he is part of that conspiracy, and he wants them to work for it. O'Brien sends Winston a copy of Goldstein's forbidden book on the secret history of Oceania which Winston and Julia read in the privacy of Mr. Charrington's room.

Shortly after waking up from a long nap, Winston and Julia hear a voice from a hidden telescreen which suddenly commands them to stand in the middle of the room. Mr. Charrington enters with a crew of stormtroopers who beat Winston and Julia, then hurry them separately away.

Part Three

Winston is tortured in jail—known as the Ministry of Love—for an interminable length of time. O'Brien is in charge of the torture. Winston confesses to various crimes, including his years of conspiracy with the ruler of Eastasia—one of the three superpowers that are often at war with Oceania. O'Brien explains to Winston that, among other things, Goldstein's book was in fact a Party creation.

It becomes clear, however, that the purpose of Miniluv is not to produce forced confessions and then kill its victims, but to "cure" the confessors, to enable them to see the truth of their confessions and the correctness of the Party's doublethink, in which "War is Peace," "Freedom is Slavery," and "Ignorance is Strength." The Party is not content with negative obedience, but must have the complete and true belief of all members. No one is executed before coming to love Big Brother.

Winston is at length able to persuade himself that the Party is right about everything—that two and two, in fact, make five—but he has not betrayed Julia, whom he still loves. At last the time comes for that step, and O'Brien sends Winston to Room 101, where each individual's darkest fear is catalogued. In Winston's case it is rats. When they threaten him with rats, he betrays Julia.

One last hurdle remains: Winston must come to love Big Brother, for the Party wanted no martyrs, no opposition at all. Winston is released a shell of a man, his hair and teeth gone, his body destroyed. He is given a small job on a committee that requires no real work. He spends most of his time in a bar, drinking oily victory gin. He sees and even speaks to Julia one day, who admits matter-of-factly that she betrayed him just as he betrayed her. They have nothing more to say to one another.

At last, it is announced over the telescreen in the bar that Oceania has won an important victory in the war. Suddenly Winston feels himself purged, no longer running with the crowd in the street but instead walking to his execution in the Ministry of Love. He can be shot now, for he at last believes. He loves Big Brother.

Characters

Big Brother

Big Brother, the mysterious all-seeing, all-knowing leader of the totalitarian society is a godlike icon to the citizens he rules. He is never seen in person, just staring out of posters and telescreens, looking stern as the caption beneath his image warns "Big Brother Is Watching You." Big Brother demands obedience and devotion of Oceania's citizens; in fact, he insists that they love him more than they love anyone else, even their own families. At the same time, he inspires fear and paranoia. His loyal followers are quick to betray anyone who seems to be disloyal to him. Through technology, Big Brother is even able to monitor the activities of people who are alone in their homes or offices.

Of course, Big Brother doesn't really exist, as is clear from the way O'Brien dodges Winston's questions about him. His image is just used by the people in power to intimidate the citizens of Oceania. Orwell meant for Big Brother to be representative of dictators everywhere, and the character was undoubtedly inspired by Adolf Hitler, Francisco Franco, Joseph Stalin, and Mao Tse-tung, all of whom were fanatically worshipped by many of their followers.

Mr. Charrington

Mr. Charrington is an acquaintance of Winston's who runs a small antique/junk shop and rents Winston a small room above it. Winston and Julia do not realize he is actually a cold, devious man and a member of the Thought Police. Charrington is responsible for Winston and Julia's eventual arrest.

Emmanuel Goldstein

Emmanuel Goldstein is the great enemy of Big Brother. An older Jewish man with white hair and a goatee, Goldstein is a former Party leader but now the head of an underground conspiracy to overthrow the Party. When his face is flashed on telescreens, people react to him as if he were the devil himself, frightening and evil. He personifies the enemy. Winston fears him yet is fascinated by him as well. He thinks Goldstein's speeches, which are broadcast as a warning against anti-Party thoughts, are transparent and shakes his head at the thought of people less intelligent and more easily led than him being taken in by such revolutionary talk. Yet Winston changes his mind later, and as he reads Goldstein's revolutionary tract, "The Theory and Practice of Oligarchical Collectivism," he is more impressed than ever by Goldstein's ideas.

Goldstein is reminiscent of Leon Trotsky, the great enemy of Soviet leader Joseph Stalin who led an unsuccessful revolt and was later brutally murdered by Stalin's men. It is no accident that he is a Jewish intellectual because dictators Stalin and Adolf Hitler deeply feared and hated the Jewish intelligentsia.

Julia

At first Winston doesn't like Julia because she seems like a zealous pro-Party advocate. Moreover, she is also a member of the Anti-Sex League, and deep down Winston resents that he will never be able to have sex with her. However, when he takes her up on her request that they meet privately, Winston discovers that Julia is smart and funny and loves sex, and she doesn't care at all about Big Brother. As for her membership in the Anti-Sex League, she is simply doing what is expected of her in society. A pretty woman with dark hair and freckles, she is basically a simple woman who doesn't worry about the revolutionary implications of her actions; she does what she does because it feels good and right. She cares little about revolution and even falls asleep when Winston is reading from Emmanuel Goldstein's revolutionary tract. Julia is practical as well. For instance, she is discreet in arranging her meetings with Winston and warns him that they will eventually get caught.

When they are caught, it is Julia who insists that her love for Winston cannot be destroyed, but she betrays Winston more quickly than he betrays her (at least, according to O'Brien), and when they finally meet again she is indifferent to him.

Katharine

Winston's wife. She was a tall, fair-haired girl, and, according to Winston, remarkably vulgar and stupid. Technically, he is still married to her, though they've lost track of each other. They parted ways about ten or eleven years before, after only fifteen months of marriage, when they realized that she could not get pregnant by him. The Party has declared that the only reason for marriage is procreation, and in fact it is illegal to have sex simply for pleasure. Therefore, there was no reason for Winston and Katharine to stay together. The Party does not believe in divorce, just separation, so Winston and Katharine just sort of drifted apart.

Readers only see Katharine through Winston's memory of her, and her main purpose in the novel is to show how the Party destroys love, sex, and loyalty between husband and wife.

O'Brien

O'Brien is a member of the Inner Party. He is a large, burly, and brutal-looking man, and yet Winston thinks he has a certain charm and civility. Winston suspects he is very intelligent and may share his subversive views of society. When O'Brien reveals that he does have revolutionary thoughts, Winston is excited to go with him to a secret underground meeting led by Emmanuel Goldstein. The group aims to overthrow the Party. Winston does not realize that O'Brien is secretly loyal to the Inner Party and that the secret underground group is simply a set-up by the Party to detect potential subversives. O'Brien betrays Winston and becomes his interrogator and torturer. It is he who reveals to Winston that the true, ugly purpose of the Party is to stay in power for power's sake. Like the Party, O'Brien cares for one thing only: power. He has no personal ambition, however. He only needs and wants to be a part of the Party's power structure.

As a torturer, O'Brien reveals himself to be extremely intelligent and sophisticated. His relationship with Winston is complicated and twisted. O'Brien seems to respect Winston, and he enjoys their conversations because Winston is a challenge. O'Brien and Winston ought to hate each other; after all, it's O'Brien's job to brainwash Winston and thereby destroy him. Still, they are drawn to each other out of respect and mutual understanding.

Old Man

Old man is a prole who lives near Winston. He remembers a lot about the past, but only insignificant snippets of his own life, so he can't answer Winston's pressing questions, such as, "Was life better then than it is now?" Winston describes him as an ant who can't see the bigger picture.

Tom Parson

Winston's neighbor, Tom Parson, is a

representative of the proletariat, or working class. His children, like children in Nazi Germany, belong to scout-like organizations sponsored by the government. They wear uniforms and are encouraged to betray their parents to the authorities should they see any signs of disloyalty. His wife, Mrs. Parsons, is about thirty but looks much older because she lives in constant fear of her own children. Tom Parsons, age 35, is sweaty, fat, pink-faced and fair-haired. He is also not very bright, a zealous man who worships the Party. Eventually, his daughter turns him in for Thought crime because he says "Down with the Party" in his sleep. He tells Winston he is grateful he was turned in before his terrible thoughts became conscious.

Prole Woman

A heavyset neighbor of Winston's, he watches her singing to herself as she hangs out the laundry. She is a symbol of the future, representing the spirit of the proletariat that cannot be crushed.

Winston Smith

Orwell named his central character Winston Smith after Winston Churchill, the Prime Minister of England during World War II; he also gave him the most common British last name, Smith. A thirty-nine-year-old man who works in the Ministry of Truth, Winston Smith is fairly ordinary. His heroism is heartfelt, not out of false notions of rebellion for the sake of power and glory. Because of the visceral nature of his actions, he acts in a foolhardy manner. For example, he keeps a diary in order to record events as he experiences them, even though he is very likely to get caught by the Thought Police. Similarly, he rents the room above a junk shop to use as a love nest with Julia despite the obvious risks. Finally, Winston trusts O'Brien, not suspecting that he is a loyal member of the Inner Party who is trying to entrap him.

Media Adaptation

- *1984* (1984), a very fine adaptation of George Orwell's infamous novel, *1984*, by director Michael Kadford, features John Hurt and Richard Burton in his final screen performance.

When he is captured and tortured, Winston

continues his defiance as long as possible. He has a strange respect for his torturer, O'Brien, and seems to enjoy their battle of intellect, ideas, and wills. Indeed, he has been thinking about and fascinated by O'Brien for years, even dreaming about him. In a way, he seems happy to be confronting him at last.

Syme

Syme, who works in the Research Department of the Ministry of Truth, is a small man with dark hair and large eyes. He is helping prepare a new dictionary of Newspeak which will eliminate even more words from the language. He is so smart and straightforward that Winston knows Syme is destined to be purged. Syme's lack of savvy and self-protectiveness irritates Winston because he knows he is loyal to Big Brother.

Winston's Mother

Dead for thirty years, Winston's mother appears only in his dreams of the past. He recalls her as a fair-haired and self-possessed woman. He's not certain what happened to her, but he thinks she was probably murdered in the purges of the 1950s (reminiscent of Joseph Stalin's infamous purges in Russia, in which large numbers of people simply disappeared overnight and were murdered). Winston misses his mother greatly and feels guilty that he survived and she did not. In fact, he has the feeling that somehow she gave her life for his.

Themes

Freedom and Enslavement/Free Will

Orwell's *1984* is set in Oceania, a totalitarian state ruled by a god-like leader named Big Brother who completely controls the citizens down to their very thoughts. Anyone who thinks subversive thoughts can be turned in by spies or by Big Brother, who monitors them through highly sensitive telescreens. If someone does not have the proper facial expression, they are considered guilty of Facecrime, so all emotions must be extremely carefully guarded. It is even possible to commit Thoughtcrime by being overheard talking in one's sleep, which Winston Smith fears will happen to him; it actually happens to his neighbor Tom Parson. Freedom exists only in the proletarian ghetto, where crime and hunger are commonplace. Winston feels he could not live in this ghetto, even though his life is almost as grim as that of the ghetto dwellers.

The punishment for even minor crimes is severe, yet people occasionally choose to break the law. The Party knows that people instinctively want to have sex, form loving bonds, and think for themselves instead of accepting unquestioningly whatever the totalitarian government tells them. As long as people choose to exercise free will, the

Party must be ever-vigilant against crime and make their punishments severe in order to remain in control.

Appearances and Reality

In totalitarian Oceania, it seems as if everyone is slavishly devoted to Big Brother and believes everything the government tells them. However, as we can understand from Winston's thoughts, all is not as it seems. Some people secretly feel and believe differently from how they behave; of course, they are extremely careful not to betray themselves. Moreover, the Party is in control of all information and revises history, even yesterday's history, to reflect their current version of events. Winston is very much aware of this, because it is his job in the inaccurately named Ministry of Truth to change the records of history. He cannot ignore what he remembers: Oceania was at war with Eurasia and allied with Eastasia yesterday, and not vice versa. If anyone else remembers differently, they certainly won't say so.

Only the old man, a powerless prole who lives on the street, speaks about what really happened in the past, but in short and irrelevant snippets about his personal experiences. It is Winston's need to reconcile what he knows with the Party's version of reality that leads to his downfall. The Party cannot allow people to have a perception of reality that is different from theirs. As Winston writes in his diary, "Freedom is the freedom to say that two plus two make four. If that is granted, all else follows."

Loyalty and Betrayal

In order to remain all-powerful, the Party destroys loyalty between people: coworkers, friends, even family members. Children are encouraged to betray their parents to the state if they suspect them of Thoughtcrimes (thinking something that goes against the Party line).

The Party has outlawed sex for pleasure and reduced marriage to an arrangement between a man and woman that exists only for procreation. Sexual urges must be repressed for fear they will lead to love, human connection, and personal loyalty, all of which threaten the Party. Winston believes that love like the love he and Julia share will eventually destroy the Party, but he underestimates the Party's ability to destroy that love and loyalty. Winston and Julia both give in to torture and betray each other. When they are released, their love and loyalty to each other has been destroyed.

Because the Party can easily detect Thoughtcrimes, people always act as if they are completely loyal to the Party. No one trusts anyone else completely. Winston makes fatal mistakes when he trusts O'Brien and Charrington, both of whom betray him. His misjudgment is almost understandable, given the subtle cues both give him to indicate that they are fellow subversives. But as it turns out, they are deliberately setting a trap for him and Julia. In the end, no one can be trusted.

Utopia and Anti-Utopia

1984 is clearly an anti-utopian book. As O'Brien tells Winston, the world he and his comrades have created is "the exact opposite of the stupid hedonistic Utopias that the old reformers imagined." Instead of being a society that is a triumph of human spirit and creativity, the society the Party has created is full of fear, torment, and treachery that will worsen over time. O'Brien gives Winston an image of the future: a boot stomping on a human face, forever and ever.

Such a pessimistic vision of the future serves a purpose, as Orwell knew. He wrote *1984* as a warning in order to make people aware that this type of society could exist if trends such as jingoism, oppression of the working class, and the erosion of language that expresses the vastness of human experience continued. Readers are supposed to see that this is only one possible future, one they must work to avoid. Orwell's anti-utopian vision captured the horrors of World War II and the fears of the cold war in the same way that earlier utopian novels, from British author Thomas More's *Utopia* to Edward Bellamy's *Looking Backward*, captured the hope and self-confidence after the end of the medieval era.

Patriotism

The blind patriotism that fueled the dictatorships of German leader Adolf Hitler and Soviet leader Joseph Stalin in the 1930s and 1940s inspired Orwell to write of Oceania and its leader, Big Brother. Just as the Germans fanatically cheered and revered Hitler, treating him as a beloved father, the citizens of Oceania look up to Big Brother as their protector, who will watch over them just as a real brother would. The huge pictures of Big Brother that can be found everywhere in Oceania are reminiscent of those of Communist leader Mao Tsetung displayed by the Chinese.

As in real totalitarian regimes, the children of Oceania play a large part in maintaining the loyalty and patriotism of the citizens. Just as German children joined the scout-like and militaristic Hitler Youth organization, the children of Oceania enjoy wearing their Junior Spies costumes, marching around, and singing patriotic songs. Orwell depicts how sinister it is for a government to use children to promote their policies when he portrays the Parsons' children as holy terrors, threatening to denounce their parents to the authorities if they don't give in to their childish demands. In the 1960s, the Chinese under Mao would indoctrinate an entire generation of children to be loyal to the state by taking them away from their parents for long periods in order to insure that the government's message could not be contradicted by the children's parents.

Topics for Further Study

- Explain how history is distorted and hidden from the citizens of Oceania. What is the result?

- Discuss how Newspeak works to alter the expression of thoughts in *1984*. Give examples from today's society of institutions and leaders that have used language to distort reality.

- Explain Winston's feelings about the proletariat, its past, present, and future.

Style

Point of View

Orwell's *1984* is told in the third person, but the point of view is clearly Winston Smith's. Through his eyes, readers are able to see how the totalitarian society functions, in particular how an individual deals with having illegal thoughts that can be detected easily by spies and telescreens that monitor one's every movement. Because readers are in Winston's head, they make the mistakes he makes in judging people. At one point he looks around a room at work and tells himself he knows just who will be vaporized within the next few years and who will be allowed to live. His percep-tions of who is a loyal party member and who is not turn out to be inaccurate, however. In this way, Orwell shows that in a paranoid society, where personal relationships with others are at best only tolerated and at worst illegal, no one can really know his fellow man.

Winston is a well-drawn character with clear opinions (clear to the reader, that is; he cannot reveal his opinions to anyone in his society). Often, critics have claimed that these opinions echo George Orwell's. For example, Winston admires the spirit of the proletariat, but looks down on them because they will never have the means or intelligence to change their lives and their government. On the other hand, he admires the sophistication of the wealthy, cultured O'Brien, even though he is an evil character. This may reflect Orwell's own class prejudices, as someone who was far more educated and worldly than most of the people from the economic class in England (the lower middle class).

Setting

Written between 1947 and 1948, *1984*'s original title was 1948, but Orwell changed it so that it would be set in the future, but still be close enough to the present to be frightening. The action takes place in London, which is now part of a country called Oceania. Oceania is one of three world superpowers, and it is continually at war with one of the other two superpowers, Eastasia and Eurasia. Enemies can change overnight and become an ally, although the Party automatically rewrites history when this happens so that no one will remember that circumstances were ever any different. This perpetual state of war consumes most of the state's resources, so city buildings are in a constant state of disrepair. All consumer goods, from food to clothing, are rationed, just as they were in England during World War II. Winston lives in what was once London, now a drab, gray, and decaying urban area.

Language and Meaning

Orwell was very aware of the power of language, so he has the totalitarian government of the future create a new language called Newspeak. Newspeak is used throughout the book by the citizens of Oceania and explained in detail in an appendix. The language is derived from Standard English and will go through many versions over the years until it reaches its final version in the year 2050. The 1984 version, however, still bears a strong resemblance to English.

The basic idea behind Newspeak is to take all words that refer to ideas the Party disagrees with and strip them of their original meaning or eliminate them entirely. The purpose of Newspeak is to narrow the range of ideas that can be expressed, so as the language develops it contains fewer and fewer words. Word forms and grammar are simplified, as is pronunciation, so that eventually the number of readers can be kept to a minimum. Newspeak also contains words to express new ideas, such as *oldthink*, which means the way people thought before the revolution. Naturally, it has a wicked and decadent connotation.

When Newspeak appeared citizens were unable to read about old ideas and express new ones that were counter to what the Party wanted them to think. An entire passage from the Declaration of Independence, "We hold these truths to be self-evident ...," can be reduced to one word: crime-think. Simplistic slogans replace more complicated ideas. The Party's most famous slogans are "War Is Peace," "Freedom Is Slavery," and "Ignorance Is Strength."

Through the device of a fictional language,

Orwell is able to point out that language can be misused to mislead people. In creating Newspeak, Orwell was influenced both by political rhetoric that takes the place of substantive communication and advertising lingo that makes ridiculous and vague promises.

Structure

1984 is divided into three parts plus an appendix. Part one sets up Winston's world, which readers see through his eyes and his thoughts. They understand his loneliness and why this leads him to take risks that will lead to his downfall.

In part two, the lengthiest part of the narrative, Winston becomes connected with people he believes are rebels like himself. He has an affair with Julia and follows O'Brien to an underground meeting of dissidents. Also in part two, Orwell includes lengthy sections from the fictional Emmanuel Goldstein's political tract. It is interesting to note that his publishers originally wanted Orwell to delete this material, because it stops the action of the narrative.

In part three, Winston and Julia have been caught by the Inner Party and separated. Winston undergoes severe torture and brainwashing at the hands of O'Brien. His dialogue and interaction with O'Brien has much dramatic tension because underlying their battle is mutual respect. Unfortunately for Winston, this respect does not translate into O'Brien freeing him. O'Brien successfully brainwashes Winston into loving Big Brother.

The book ends with an appendix on the development and structure of the language called "Newspeak." The appendix is written as if it were a scholarly article, and while it serves to clarify the use of Newspeak in the novel it is interesting to note that the publisher originally wanted to cut it, thinking it unnecessary.

Totalitarianism

In 1948, when Orwell's *1984* was published, World War II had just ended. One of England's allies had been Russia, which was ruled by a despotic dictator named Joseph Stalin. Stalin ruled with an iron fist, and was famous for his midnight purges: he would round up hundreds of citizens at a time and murder them in deserted areas, much as Oceania citizens are "vaporized." Stalin's victims were his imagined enemies, such as political dissidents, artists, or Jews. Meanwhile, Adolf Hitler, in Germany, had slaughtered his enemies as well, in the end killing six million Jews plus nine million Slavs, gypsies, political dissidents, homosexuals, and mentally challenged people. Mao Tse-tung in China was fighting for communism against Chinese nationalist forces under Chiang Kai-shek. Mao would finally defeat the nationalists in 1949 and begin a long, oppressive totalitarian regime.

Other dictators of the time included Francisco Franco in Spain and Benito Mussolini in Italy. These oppressive rulers controlled citizens through propaganda and violence. This state of affairs prompted Orwell to create Big Brother, the ultimate totalitarian leader who dominates all political, social, and economic activities.

Socialism and Communism

Orwell fought against Franco in the Spanish Civil War in the mid-1930s, supporting the socialist left. He was not a communist, but a dedicated Democratic socialist who believed that the government, not private enterprise, should control the production and distribution of goods, and as such he was greatly concerned about the lives of the poor and working class.

All over the world, throughout the twentieth century, working class people had been fighting for better lives. In America, workers fought a long and hard battle for labor reforms that would eventually include such benefits as job security, safety regulation, overtime and hazardous duty pay, vacation and sick days, health insurance, pensions, disability, and child labor laws, which modern workers sometimes take for granted. Some U.S. and British workers turned to socialism and communism, thinking that perhaps these alternate forms of economic and social structure would solve their problems. In the late nineteenth century, Karl Marx of Germany proposed that to resolve the gross inequality between the workers and the bosses, the working class, or proletariat, would have to revolt and establish a new communist regime in which one authoritarian party would control the political and economic systems. He believed workers ought to own their farms and factories and distribute the profits evenly among workers.

Here in America, the capitalist factory and

mine owners eventually conceded to labor's demands and the socialists and communists were marginalized. This act deferred American workers from revolting against their government. Communist revolutions did occur in Russia and in China, but eventually those countries modified their economic systems.

America's response to communism was extreme during the Cold War era of the 1950s; in fact, many people believed the U.S. government was acting just as oppressively as communist governments were. Under the leadership of Senator Joe McCarthy, the House (of Representatives) Committee on Un-American Activities aggressively attacked public figures who were suspected communists, demanding that they name other communists or be blackballed in their industries. Hollywood writers and filmmakers were especially hard hit by the mania and many careers were destroyed before President Truman and public opinion turned against McCarthy and the witch hunt ended. The paranoia that characterized the McCarthy era was similar to the paranoia in *1984*, as people were pressured to betray their friends, co-workers, and even parents in order to save themselves. Today, communism still has some followers in the United States and England, as does Democratic socialism, which Orwell embraced wholeheartedly.

Television

Aside from being concerned about labor and government, Orwell was very aware of an important invention that was just becoming popular after World War II and would eventually be a dominant force in Western culture: the television. The first BBC broadcast in Britain occurred in 1937, and TV was first demonstrated to the American public in 1939 at the New York World's Fair. Television's popularity grew enormously throughout the 1950s, and today 98% of American households own at least one color television set. Orwell recognized the enormous potential of this communication tool, which would soon be in every home. He imagined that the television could one day not only broadcast propaganda nonstop but that it could transmit back images of action in front of the screen, allowing the broadcaster to spy on its viewers.

Compare & Contrast

- **1948:** West Berlin, Germany, is blockaded by the Soviets. The Americans begin an airlift to help the stranded Berliners.

  1984: The Berlin wall, built in 1961 to keep East Germans from defecting to the West, remains in place.

  Today: East and West Germany are reunified, after the Berlin wall was taken down in 1990.

- **1948/49:** Mao Tse-tung battles Chiang Kai-shek and his nationalist forces, finally defeating them in 1949 and establishing a totalitarian communist regime.

  1984: China has survived the severe cultural purging of the Great Proletarian Cultural Revolution in the 1960s. Opened to the West in the 1970s because of President Nixon's visit in 1972, China is now trading with the West and incorporating some small democratic and economic reforms.

  Today: In 1989, students demanding greater economic and civil rights reforms protested in Tiananmen Square in Beijing and were gunned down by Chinese troops. China continues to trade with the West, but its democratic movement has been slowed considerably.

- **1948/49:** In September, 1949, President Truman announces that Russia, too, has the atom bomb, having developed the technology on its own.

  1984: In 1991 the Cold War continues as the arms race between the Soviet Union and the United

States escalates.

Today: On December 8, 1987, President Ronald Reagan and Soviet leader Mikhail Gorbachev sign an agreement to dismantle all 1,752 U.S. and 859 Soviet nuclear missiles within a 300 to 3,400-mile range. In 1991 the former Soviet Republic breaks up. American investors are helping the Soviets establish new businesses as the Soviets concentrate their attention on revamping their economy.

- **1949:** There are one million television sets in the United States and two dozen TV stations. There will be ten million TV sets by 1951, fifty million by 1959.

1984: Eighty-five million U.S. households own a television set. Cable television reaches almost half of those households. Computers start to become a household product in the United States with approximately 13% or 516,750 computers owned by consumers.

Today: Ninety-eight percent of U.S. households (95 million homes) own a color television set, 28 percent own three or more televisions, 65 percent have cable access. New TV technology on the horizon includes high-definition television. In 1995, over three million people owned a personal computer. Use of a vast computer network, called the Internet, which originated in the 1960s and connects users from over 160 countries to each other via electronic mail, exploded during the 1990s with an estimated count of 20 to 30 million users in mid-1995.

Critical Overview

When *1984* was published, critics were impressed by the sheer power of George Orwell's grim and horrifying vision of the future. They praised Orwell's gripping prose, which captured so well the details of life under an oppressive regime, from the tasteless, sodden public meals Winston eats to the gritty dust of the gray streets. In 1949, critic Mark Shorer wrote in his *New York Times Book Review* essay that "No real reader can neglect this experience with impunity.... He will be asked to read through pages of sustained physical and psychological pain that have seldom been equaled and never in such quiet, sober prose." In the same year, British novelist V. S. Pritchett wrote his reaction to the novel in *New Statesman and Nation.* "I do not think," the critic concluded, "I have ever read a novel more frightening and depressing; and yet, such are the originality, the suspense, the speed of writing and withering indignation that it is impossible to put the book down."

Critics also praised Orwell's ability to provoke moral outrage at Oceania, a society that so completely destroys the human values many people hold dear, from love to art.

Because *1984* was published during the reign of Russian leader Joseph Stalin, a former ally of England and the United States who was proving to be a cruel and violent dictator, critics of the time believed that the novel was about the events in the Soviet Union. Some mistakenly believed that by setting the story in England, Orwell meant to criticize British socialism, particularly since he names the Inner Party Ingsoc ("ENGlish SOCialism"). Orwell strongly denied this. Then again, some critics saw the novel as a satire of the contemporary social and political scene. Certainly, many of Orwell's details bear a resemblance to life in London post-World War II. However, over time critics came to realize that Orwell meant the story to be a universal warning about the dangers of any totalitarian dictatorship.

Sources

Elaine Hoffman Baruch, "The Golden Country: Sex and Love in *1984*," in *"1984" Revisited: Totalitarianism in Our Century*, Harper & Row, 1983, pp. 47-56.

Robert Christgau, "Writing for the People," in *The Village Voice*, February 1, 1983, pp. 54-5.

Martin Esslin, "Television and Telescreen," in *On Nineteen Eighty-Four*, edited by Peter Stansky, W. H. Freeman & Co., 1983, pp. 126-38.

Irving Howe, "*1984:* Enigmas of Power," in *1984 Revisited: Totalitarianism in Our Century*, edited by Irving Howe, Harper & Row, 1983, pp. 3-18.

Marcus Smith, "The Wall of Blackness: A Psychological Approach to *1984*," in *Modern Fiction Studies*, Winter, 1968–69, pp. 42-33.

Ian Watt, "Winston Smith: The Last Humanist," in *On Nineteen Eighty-Four*, W. H. Freeman, 1983, pp. 103-13.

For Further Study

Paul Chilton and Aubrey Crispin, editors, *Nineteen Eighty-Four in 1984*, Comedia Publishing Group, 1983.

> Collection of essays focusing on the relevance of Orwell's novel in contemporary political and social life.

College Literature, Vol. XI, No. 1, 1984, pp. 1-113.

> Issue devoted to studies of *1984*.

Miriam Gross, editor, *The World of George Orwell*, Simon & Schuster, 1972.

> Collection of critical and biographical essays.

Alfred Kazin, "Not One of Us," in *The New York Review of Books*, Vol. XXXI, no. 10, June 14, 1984, pp. 13-4, 16, 18.

> Kazin discusses the political nature of Orwell's novel.

Modern Fiction Studies, Vol. 21, No. 1, Spring 1975, pp. 3-136.

> Issue devoted to Orwell criticism.

Erica Munk, "Love Is Hate: Women and Sex in *1984*," in *Village Voice*, Vol. XXVIII, No. 5, February 1, 1983, pp. 50-2.

Munk criticizes Orwell novel for its inattention to the roles (or lack thereof) of women in Oceania.

Norman Podhoretz, "If Orwell Were Alive Today," in *Harper's*, Vol. 266, No. 1592, January, 1983, pp. 30-2, 34-7.

Podhoretz, using the text of *1984* as evidence, claims Orwell for the neo-conservatives.

Ian Watt, "Winston Smith: The Last Humanist," in *On Nineteen Eighty-Four*, edited by Peter Stansky, W. H. Freeman & Co. 1983, pp. 103-13.

Watt describes Winston Smith as a humanist and his destruction at the hands of the Party as the destruction of the values of humanism.

George Woodcock, *Remembering Orwell*, edited by Stephen Wadhams, Penguin, 1984.

Woodcock disagrees with writers such as Podhoretz who claim Orwell for the neo-conservatives, placing him instead in a line of English literary radicals including Jonathan Swift and Charles Dickens.

CPSIA information can be obtained
at www.ICGtesting.com
Printed in the USA
BVHW011136140822
R13930800001B/R139308PG644458BVX00001B/1